LIGHTS

A FABLE ABOUT HANUKAH

Gesher / Jerusalem Productions Presents

A FABLE ABOUT HANUKAH

Based on Gesher's Animated Television Special

Illustrated by Noam Nadav
Backgrounds by Miriam Katin
Graphics by Diane Liff

LIGHTS

by
YEHUDA and SARA
WURTZEL

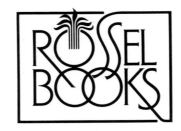

Chappaqua, New York

Library of Congress Cataloging in Publication Data

Wurtzel, Yehuda.
    Lights : a fable about Hanukah, based on Gesher's
animated television special.

    Summary: The people of Jerusalem, under great
duress, manage to keep their lights from destruction
by Greek invaders.
    1. Hanukkah--Juvenile literature. [1. Hanukkah]
I. Wurtzel, Sara. II. Nadav, Noam, ill. III. Gesher/
Jerusalem Productions. IV. Lights (Motion picture)
V. Title.
BM695.H3W87 1984   296.4'35   84-18297
ISBN 0-940646-55-2
ISBN 0-940646-56-0 (pbk.)

The film "LIGHTS" was made possible through the support of

The Joint Program for Jewish Education of
— The State of Israel Ministry of Education and Culture
— The Jewish Agency for Israel
— The World Zionist Organization

Published by ROSSEL BOOKS
44 Dunbow Drive,
Chappaqua NY 10514
(914) 238-8954

Gesher/Jerusalem Productions
421 Seventh Avenue, Suite 905
New York, N.Y. 10001, U.S.A.
Tel. 212-564-0338

LIGHTS is written in the form of a fable or allegory, but the miracles of Hanukah and the events surrounding them are no less true for being told this way. The purpose of an allegory, after all, is not to simply record history, but to try to illuminate what historical events may mean. . . .

לאורות שלנו —

יצחק נ״י

אליהו נ״י

יעקב ישראל נ״י

שמחה נ״י ו...

״וראה בנים לבניך

שלום על — ישראל״ תהלים קכ״ח

מאבא ואמא

Long ago in the wilderness, at a mountain called Sinai...

... the lights first came down to earth, carrying secrets to the people waiting below.

... Though hundreds of years passed, the
lights never stopped sparkling and speaking.

And when the people settled in their land and built their cities, they brought the lights with them.

The Lights made themselves right at home in Jerusalem.
They always had something new to tell...

... about how people could live with one another in happiness and fairness.

Even at home, there was no part of life that the lights didn't touch and brighten.

And in the heart of Jerusalem the people had a special place for the lights. It was in a golden tree with seven branches, called the *Menorah*.

Then, one day, ships came over the sea.

Alexander the Great and the armies of Greece set out to unite the whole world.

They found the Persians first.

Soon there were no more Persians left to fight...

... and Alexander decided to march against Jerusalem!

The people of Jerusalem were living quietly with their lights...

... when suddenly they heard the sounds of Alexander's army approaching the city!

Unarmed, the keeper of the lights, the High Priest, went out
to meet the mighty army...

... and Alexander saw something that made him change his mind about conquering the city. So, there was no battle after all. Alexander and his armies entered Jerusalem in peace.

Alexander was fascinated by the mysterious lights. He studied them and tried to make them behave according to all the laws he knew. ... but they were determined to be themselves.

Meanwhile, the Greeks made themselves right at home in
Jerusalem. They showed the people there all kinds of new and
interesting things... their science, music, art, philosophy, language...

...even their sports seemed, well... beautiful in the eyes of the people of the city.

Time passed, Alexander the Great was gone, and the new Greeks who ruled over Jerusalem didn't care for the lights very much.

So some of the people decided they would be better off without their lights....

After all, without lights they could be part of the Greek world of wealth and power.

They even tried to dress like the Greeks, to talk like them, to imitate them in every way.

Only one thing stood between some of the people of Jerusalem and their wish to be just like the Greeks...

In time, the new Greek rulers decided that the lights were too independent ... too different to be allowed to sparkle within their empire.

So the Greeks planned to get rid of the lights... but in a way that wouldn't cause too much trouble... or so they thought.

They tried to persuade the people that replacing their lights with shiny new letters was the thing to do!

But when that didn't work, the Greeks began to take away
the lights by force.

Soon the lights weren't safe anywhere...

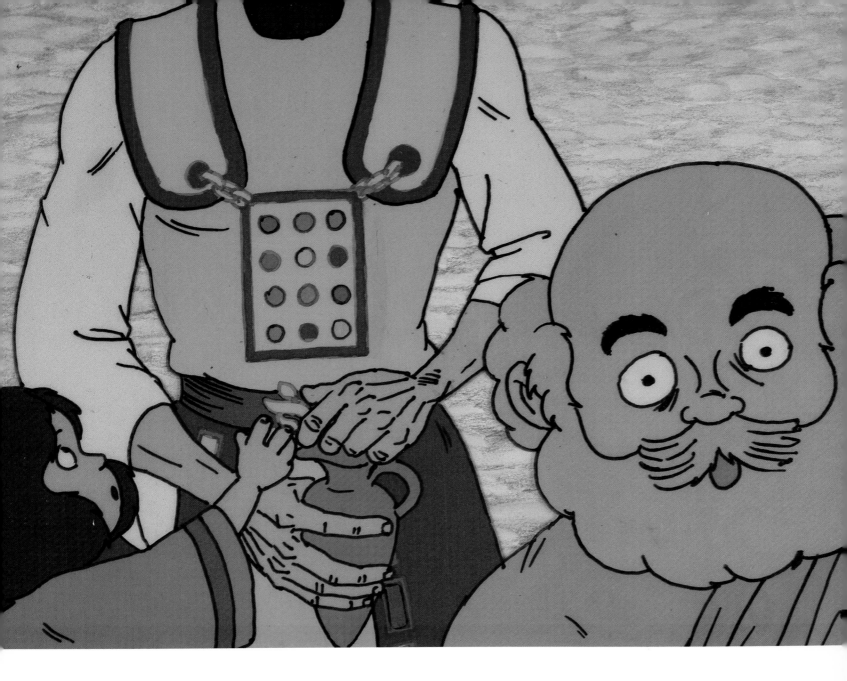

... but the people managed to keep one little light alive.

When the Greeks saw that they couldn't convince the people
to give up the lights, they decided to get rid of the people instead.

The people of Jerusalem were forced to flee into the hills.

But Greek soldiers pursued them there...

... and attacked!

The people fought back ... every one of them. The Greeks
hadn't expected such fierce resistance.

Their armies marched off in defeat.

When the people returned to their city, they found the *Menorah* fallen, cold, and empty, with no lights to fill it.

They searched everywhere for their lights.

Just when it seemed that the lights had been lost...

... one small jar was found!

The golden *Menorah* was rekindled...

... and the lights sparkled in Jerusalem once more.

And so, every year...

... at the time when these things happened...

... there's a Festival of Lights.

There's a Festival of Lights because the people kept the lights...

... and treasured them.

LIGHTING THE HANUKAH LIGHTS

Each evening of the 8 days of Hanukah, from the time the sun sets, we light the Hanukah Lights. On the first evening: one candle (or wick burning in olive oil.) On the second evening two flames are lit, and so on, adding one more light each night until 8 lights burn on the last night of Hanukah.

Before the light(s) are kindled, two blessings are said, one on the lights, and one on the miracles. They are:

בָּרוּךְ אַתָּה יְיָ אֱלֹהֵינוּ מֶלֶךְ הָעוֹלָם, אֲשֶׁר קִדְּשָׁנוּ בְּמִצְוֹתָיו וְצִוָּנוּ לְהַדְלִיק נֵר שֶׁל חֲנֻכָּה:

Blessed be You, O *God* our God, King of the Universe, Who has sanctified us by His commandments and commanded us to kindle the Hanukah lights.

בָּרוּךְ אַתָּה יְיָ אֱלֹהֵינוּ מֶלֶךְ הָעוֹלָם, שֶׁעָשָׂה נִסִּים לַאֲבוֹתֵינוּ בַּיָּמִים הָהֵם בַּזְּמַן הַזֶּה:

Blessed be You, O *God* our God, King of the Universe, Who performed miracles for our fathers in those days, at this season.

On the first night of Hanukah, the blessing on the season is also said:

בָּרוּךְ אַתָּה יְיָ אֱלֹהֵינוּ מֶלֶךְ הָעוֹלָם, שֶׁהֶחֱיָנוּ וְקִיְּמָנוּ וְהִגִּיעָנוּ לַזְּמַן הַזֶּה:

Blessed be You O *God* our God, King of the Universe, Who has kept us in life and sustained us and enabled us to reach this season.

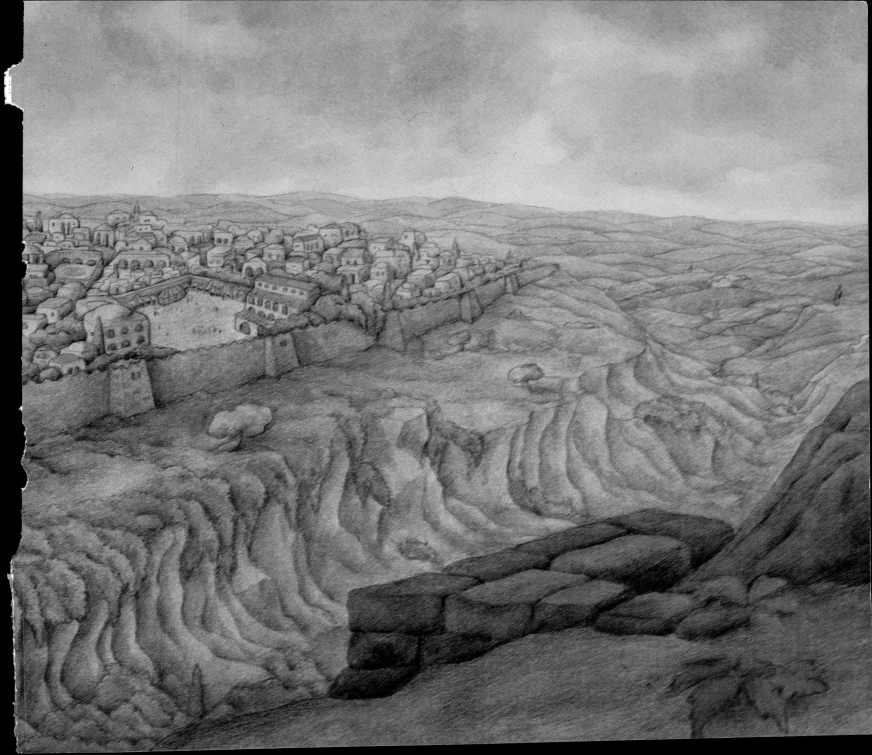